KOALAS

AUSTRALIAN ANIMAL DISCOVERY LIBRARY

Lynn M. Stone

Rourke Corporation, Inc.
Vero Beach, Florida 32964

PHOTO CREDITS

All photos © Lynn M. Stone

ACKNOWLEDGEMENTS

The author thanks the following for photographic assistance:
Lone Pine Koala Sanctuary, Brisbane, Queensland, Australia

LIBRARY OF CONGRESS
Library of Congress Cataloging-in-Publication Data
Stone, Lynn M.
    Koalas / by Lynn M. Stone.

    p. cm. — (Australian animal discovery library)
    Summary: Describes the physical characterists, behavior,
natural habitat, and relationship to humans of the marsupial
that looks like a teddy bear.
    ISBN 0-86593-055-4
    1. Koala—Juvenile literature. [1. Koala.]
I. Title. II. Series: Stone, Lynn M. Australian animal discovery
library.
QL737.M384S76   1990
599.2—dc20   90-30487
                              CIP
                              AC

Printed in the USA

TABLE OF CONTENTS

THE KOALA

The cute, cuddly koala *(Phascolarctos cinereus)* of Australia has won hearts all over the world. Koalas are often called "teddy bears."

The furry koala does look like a teddy, but it is not a bear. Actually the koala is a **marsupial.**

Female marsupials have a pocket of skin called a **pouch.** Like other marsupials, the female koala uses her pouch to raise her baby.

Marsupials give birth to tiny, helpless babies. They need the covering of a warm pouch.

Koala in Eucalyptus

THE KOALA'S COUSINS

Scientists have included all the world's pouched mammals as marsupials. Altogether there are 258 kinds of marsupials, including kangaroos and opossums.

None of the other marsupials is a close relative of the koala. It is by itself in one of the 16 families of marsupials.

The koala's nearest relative is the wombat, which also lives in Australia. Wombats and koalas have backward-facing pouches and almost no tail.

The koala's only marsupial cousin in North America is the opossum.

Virginia Opossum

HOW THEY LOOK

Koalas have soft, thick fur. The fur is gray or brown with some white trim.

A koala has a large, round nose and big, round, fur-trimmed ears. It certainly looks like a teddy bear.

A koala is from 23 to 33 inches long. It can weigh from nine to 33 pounds. Most often a koala weighs 18 to 23 pounds.

Koalas in southern Australia are larger and heavier usually than koalas in northern Australia.

Koala in Eucalyptus

WHERE THEY LIVE

Koalas live only in Australia. They are found from the southeast part of Queensland south through east New South Wales and Victoria to southeast South Australia.

Their **habitat,** or home, is **eucalyptus** forest. The forest may be on a mountain, along the sea, or along a river.

About 600 kinds of eucalyptus trees grow in Australia. They are unlike any of the wild trees in North America.

The koala eats only about 35 kinds of eucalyptus. It leaves the others.

Koala in Eucalyptus

HOW THEY LIVE

A koala isn't much of a world traveler. In fact, a koala hardly gets around its own neighborhood!

Koalas spend almost their entire lives in trees. At night they eat in trees. By day they sleep in trees. Now and then they shuffle down one tree and shinny up another.

Several koalas may live in the same area. Each koala, however, claims its own tree. A koala marks the tree with scent from a **gland** on its chest.

Koala showing scent gland

THE KOALA'S BABIES

A koala baby, before it is born, lives in its mother for just 35 days. It weighs less than one-half ounce when it is born. (Koalas rarely have twins.)

The baby koala lives in its mother's pouch for six months after it is born. It spends another six months staying close to mom. Baby koalas often cling to their mothers' back.

A koala doesn't reach full size until it is four or five years old.

Koalas in captivity have reached 20 years of age.

Koala with baby

PREDATOR AND PREY

Animals which eat only plants are called **herbivores.** The koala is a herbivore. But koalas don't eat just any plant. A lettuce and tomato salad would not interest a koala.

A koala lives almost entirely on eucalyptus leaves. With its clawed toes, the koala can climb high into a eucalyptus. It has a keen nose for telling the kinds of eucalyptus that it likes.

A koala high in a eucalyptus tree is quite safe. Very few are **prey,** or food, for **predators.** Predators are hunting animals, like dingoes and goanna lizards, that eat other animals.

Koala feeding

THE KOALA AND PEOPLE

Being cute hasn't always helped protect the koala. In the early 20th century, the koalas were killed by the millions.

Koala fur was in demand. It was warm, beautiful, and long-lasting. By 1924, over two million koala skins had been shipped from Australia to other countries.

The koala was clearly in trouble. Still, the Australian state of Queensland allowed another 600,000 koalas to be killed in 1927.

The 1920's almost made the koala **extinct,** gone forever. Just before it was too late, many people spoke out against the killing of koalas.

Lone Pine Koala Sanctuary,
Queensland

THE KOALA'S FUTURE

After 1927, Australia began to protect its koalas. Koalas began to multiply again. Koalas were moved into places where they had been wiped out.

Today the koala remains protected. In some parts of Australia it is again common. In other places, however, koala habitat is being destroyed. When koala habitat and its "brands" of eucalyptus disappear, the koala does too.

All of the forests cannot be saved. Just as koalas need forests, so do the people of Australia. Hopefully there will always be some forest saved for Australia's favorite animal.

Glossary

eucalyptus (u kal IP tus)—a family of evergreen trees found mostly in Australia

extinct (ex TINKT)—the point at which an animal species no longer exists, such as the quagga

gland (GLAND)—one of many bag-like body organs that store, and sometimes release, liquid of some kind

habitat (HAB a tat)—the kind of place an animal lives in, such as a forest

herbivore (ERB a vore)—an animal which eats plants

marsupial (mar SOOP ee ul)—a family of mammals in which the females have a pouch for raising the young, which are born not fully formed

pouch (POWCH)—the mother marsupial's warm pocket of skin in which her baby is raised

predator (PRED a tor)—an animal that kills other animals for food

prey (PRAY)—an animal that is hunted by another for food

INDEX